Wonder Stories
READING LEVEL 2

REM 467

COVER DESIGNED BY: **Don Merrifield**

A TEACHING RESOURCE FROM

REMEDIA PUBLICATIONS

To find Remedia products in a store near you, visit:
www.rempub.com/stores

REMEDIA PUBLICATIONS, INC.
7900 EAST GREENWAY ROAD • SUITE 110 • SCOTTSDALE, AZ • 85260

RESEARCH-BASED ACTIVITIES
Supports State & National Standards

This product utilizes innovative strategies and proven methods to improve student learning. The product is based upon reliable research and effective practices that have been replicated in classrooms across the United States. Information regarding the Common Core State Standards this product meets is available at www.rempub.com/standards

INTRODUCTION

Wonder Stories is a series of books designed to improve the reading comprehension of older students whose reading abilities are below grade level. The series is also ideal for challenging the abilities of younger students functioning at or above grade level.

Each factual article begins with a question about a topic that has prompted thoughts like, "I wonder how, I wonder why, I wonder what. . ." Comprehension questions following each story address the following skills: main idea, finding a fact, locating an answer, inference, vocabulary, and word analysis.

The high-interest stories appeal to all ages, making it possible to tailor the appropriate book for individual students depending upon their reading abilities. In order to ensure that stories were at the desired reading levels, readability scales were used.*

CONTENTS

A Note About Readability Scores

Readability scales are useful as long as one realizes their limitations. Results are approximate guidelines only, with a minimum margin of error of (+ or −) 1.5 grade levels. In other words, a story measured at a second grade readability level could easily be suitable for both first and third graders. Another limitation is that two different readability scales can be applied to the same sample, yet yield widely varied results. In spite of the inexact nature of readability scales, we at Remedia use them because they measure word and sentence length, both valid predictors of readability. They also help us provide vocabulary-controlled materials in order to meet the special education needs of many of our valued clients. At the same time, we realize that these scales are not designed to measure every other factor affecting readability, such as sentence structure or appeal to the reader. We are also aware of the variance in standards and expectations set for each grade level. What is first grade material in one school may be second grade in another. At Remedia we strive to take all these factors into consideration as we develop and revise materials. We leave the rest in your capable hands. Regarding readability, you—and your students—will be the final judge.

Name _____

What causes colds?

For years no one knew why we catch colds. Most colds attack in the winter. For that reason, we thought chilly air gave us colds. Now we know that colds come from a kind of germ. The germ is a virus.

The first sign of a cold is often a sore throat. The viruses make themselves at home there. Then they move down into your chest. Or they may move up into your nose and head. You start to sneeze and cough. Your eyes may water, and you may feel sleepy.

There is no cure for the cold. A cold will go away by itself in three to seven days. The best thing is to rest and drink fruit juices.

If you sneeze, be sure to cover your nose and mouth. Otherwise the germs will spread. All your friends might get the germ.

After you have a cold, you are protected from that virus. It won't hurt you again. But you can catch a second cold from a different virus.

1. This story is about why we watch _____ .

2. What are the signs of a cold? _____
    _____

3. Write the sentence in paragraph one that tells what kind of germ turns into a cold.
    _____

4. Who might you go see if you have a cold?
    _____

5. What is a word in paragraph five that means "kept safe from"?
    _____

6. Write the homonyms in the story for these words:

    knows: _____   heir: _____

    soar: _____

Why do you sleep?

Your body likes to stay active. On a normal day, you might ride your bike to school. Later, you might play softball. Then you might walk to the store for some juice.

But, at some point, your body needs to rest. It begins to weaken. You don't have the same amount of energy. This happens because your body must have food and sleep each day. Without these, your cells slow down. You can't perform.

You know when you are sleepy. Your eyes feel heavy. You want to lie down. You lose interest in what is happening around you.

While you sleep, your muscles have time to get stronger. But your brain does not rest. It thinks about what happened that day. It also dreams. Your brain does all kinds of things that you don't remember the next day.

After eight hours of sleep, you feel ready to go again. You are refreshed.

If you don't get sleep, you feel grouchy. You might also start to see things that aren't really there. That is your body's way of saying, "Stop! I need a break."

1. This story is about why our bodies need to _____ .

2. What happens to your muscles while you sleep?

    _____

3. Which paragraph tells what your brain does while you sleep? _____

4. What do you think would happen if you kept playing softball even though you needed sleep?

    _____

    _____

5. What is a word in paragraph six that means "upset; not in a good mood"?

    _____

6. Find a three-syllable word in each of these paragraphs:

    paragraph two: _____   paragraph four: _____

2

Name _____

How many bones do you have?

Believe it or not, the number of bones in your body changes as you grow! At certain times, you have more bones than at other times.

You are born with 270 bones. As a baby, your bones are quite small. In fact, some of them look more like twigs in size. These are called bony centers. They are just pieces of bones.

As you grow, new bony centers form. Soon you have 443 bones and bony centers. At that point, they start to join together. Two or more will grow into one strong bone.

By the time you become a teen, you will have lost your bony centers. You will have only 206 bones. That's less than you had at birth.

The changing of bones never stops. But it does slow down. An old person will still lose bones. A 90-year-old grandmother may have fewer than 200 bones left.

1. This story is about how many _____ you have as you grow.

2. At what point in life do you have the fewest bones?

   _____

3. Write the sentence in paragraph two that tells how many bones you have when you are born.

   _____

4. Why do you think it's important for your bones to grow?

   _____

5. What is a word in paragraph two that means "small sticks"?

   _____

6. Write two other forms of the word "bone."

   _____

Why are teeth hard?

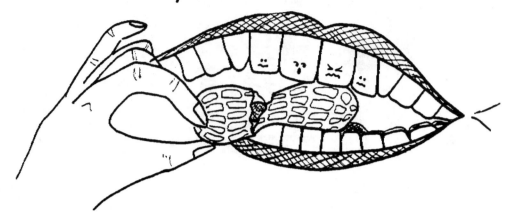

Think of all the things you eat. Maybe you crack peanut shells with your teeth. Or maybe you eat crunchy chips. Burgers need plenty of chewing.

Each time your teeth bite down, they create pressure. This pressure equals hundreds of pounds. It's as though a hammer were pounding the food.

If your teeth weren't strong, they would crack. Broken bones can mend. But cracked teeth can't fix themselves. Yet your teeth are harder than your bones!

Your teeth stay strong with a special coating. It is called enamel. It protects the inside of your teeth, called the pulp. The pulp is what hurts when your dentist drills.

To keep your teeth healthy, you must brush them. This removes small bits of food. If you don't brush, the food turns into plaque. Plaque sticks to your teeth. It attracts germs. The germs make acids, which cling to your teeth. That is how cavities are formed.

To keep your teeth hard and healthy, brush them each day. Stay away from eating too many sweets. If you don't, you might end up with a toothache.

1. This story is about how teeth stay _____ and _____.

2. What special coating is good for teeth, and which coating is bad?

    _____

3. Write the sentence in paragraph three that tells how hard your teeth are.

    _____

    _____

4. How do you think cavities can be repaired? _____

    _____

5. What is a word in paragraph two that means "strong force"?_____

6. Write two compound words found in paragraph one.

    _____

Name _____

Why do you have a heart?

Your heart is a muscle. It has one big job to do. It must send blood to each part of your body. It does this every minute of the day. Even when you sleep, your heart pumps blood.

When you rest, your heart beats about once a second. That is about 60 beats a minute. Some hearts beat faster or slower. When you run, your heart speeds up. Your body needs more blood for exercise.

For a tiny part of each second, your heart takes a rest. Add up all those rests. They total about five hours of rest a day.

If blood were water, your heart could fill a lake. It pumps about 250 million quarts of blood in a lifetime. In one day, it pumps 10,000 quarts.

All your muscles need special care. So does your heart. You must learn to take care of it. Eat foods that are low in fat. Get some exercise every day. Then your heart will stay strong.

1. This story is about a muscle called the _____ .

2. What is the main job of your heart?

    _____

3. Which paragraph tells how to take good care of your heart? _____

4. What does your heart do for about 19 hours of each day?

    _____

5. What is a word in paragraph five that means "actions your body does to keep it strong"?

    _____

6. Write the forms of these words that mean "more."

    fast: _____

    slow: _____

Why do you sneeze?

You must breathe air to live. Air enters your body through your nose. Then it goes to your lungs. Dust and dirt float through the air. They should not be allowed into your lungs. Other things, like bugs, are too big and could clog your lungs.

Your nose catches all these unwanted particles. Sometimes this makes your nose tickle. A quick rush of air is forced out of your lungs. It is called a sneeze.

Sneezing clears your nose. It sends germs away, too. If you cover your nose and mouth with a tissue, the germs won't spread.

Some people can't be around certain grass, food, or even animals. These things make them sneeze. These people have allergies. That means their bodies don't act well when unwanted particles are near. People can also have allergies to milk, eggs, soap, and nuts.

1. This story is about the reasons why you _____ .

2. What role does your nose play in sneezing? _____

    _____

3. Write the sentence in paragraph one that tells what things float through the air.

    _____

4. What is the most important thing to do if you have an allergy?

    _____

5. What is a word in paragraph one that means "to block"?

    _____

6. What is a compound word in paragraph two?

    _____

6

Name _____

How do broken bones heal?

Babies have very soft bones. As they get older, the bones receive calcium. This makes them stronger. Bones stop growing bigger by the time a person is 18. But the bones keep growing new cells.

This supply of new cells heals a broken bone. If a person breaks an arm, cells start to grow around the break. This happens right away. Soon, these cells reach out to each other. In time, they connect. They form a kind of web. In a few weeks or months, the place where the cells connect becomes solid again.

However, this growth must be helped along. Otherwise, the bones will not grow together in a straight line. That is why doctors put casts on broken arms and legs. The casts are made from plaster. Then they are covered with gauze. Casts keep the broken bones from moving around. Then they can grow back the right way. They become as good as new.

1. This story is about how a broken bone _____ .

2. What keeps growing in bones all our lives? _____

3. Which paragraph tells how casts help broken bones? _____

4. What could happen if a broken bone did not grow together in a straight line?

_____

5. What is a word in paragraph two that means the bones "join together"?

_____

6. Write all the plural words in this sentence: That is why doctors put casts on broken arms and legs.

_____

Why do you have hair and nails?

    Hair and nails protect your body. For example, hair keeps your head warm. This is important. Most of your body heat is lost through your head in the winter. But hair keeps your whole body warmer by protecting your head. It also helps prevent bumps and bruises.

    Hair in the nose keeps dust out of your lungs. Eyebrows keep sweat out of your eyes. Eyelashes can feel tiny objects that might hurt your eyes. If lashes are touched, they tell you to close your eyes quickly.

    Nails also protect you. They guard the tips of your fingers and toes from sharp things. Nails also help you grab small objects. If you play the piano, your nails may grow faster. The pressure on your fingertips makes them grow.

    Hair and nails have more in common. They are both made of layers of soft cells under the skin. By the time you see hair or nails appear, they have become dead cells.

1. This story is about how hair and nails _____ your body.

2. What do eyebrows do for you?

    _____

3. Write the sentence in paragraph one that tells how we lose most of our body heat.

    _____

4. Besides having hair, how can you try to not lose body heat from your head during the winter?

    _____

5. What is a word in paragraph three that means "strong force"?

    _____

6. What is a homonym for "hare"? _____

Name _____

What animals like night more than day?

Animals that hunt in the dark like night more than day. Owls and bats are two of these animals.

Owls find their best meals at night. They like to dine on mice and other small critters. Owls have great eyesight in dark or light. They have very large eyes that are sharp. They also hear well. An owl can hear the pitter-patter of a mouse's footsteps on the ground!

Owls have very soft feathers over their wings. This helps them to fly with hardly a sound. The poor mouse doesn't know it's about to become dinner. The owl grabs it with his claws and carries it away.

Bats don't see as well as owls. You may have heard the words, "blind as a bat." Bats are not blind. But they use their ears to help them catch their food.

As a bat flies, it makes a squeaky chirp. The sound of it bounces off nearby objects. Then the sound returns to the bat, like an echo. The echo tells the bat that something is near. It might be the insects that the bat likes for a snack. This handy echo system also keeps the bat from running into things while it flies.

1. This story is about two animals that like the night. They are _____ and _____.

2. What do owls eat?_____

3. Which paragraph tells how well bats can see?

    _____

4. What traits do you think mice have to help them escape from owls?

    _____

5. What is a word in paragraph five that means "useful or practical"?

    _____

6. Write two compound words in paragraph two.

    _____

Name _____

Why do birds lose their feathers?

Have you ever seen loose feathers on the ground? Maybe you thought a bird had been hurt. Most likely the bird was supposed to lose those feathers. This is called molting. Birds molt whether they live indoors or outdoors.

To a bird, feathers are its only clothes. In time, the feathers wear out. They need a new set now and then. Lucky for the birds, they don't have to buy new clothes. They just grow them.

This usually happens at the end of summer. That is the molting season. The bird doesn't lose all its feathers at once. If it did, it couldn't fly. Only a few at a time come out. New ones quickly replace the old.

A mother eagle will pull out her own feathers to line her nest. So will some smaller birds. The feathers make the nest soft for the babies. You may find some of these loose feathers near trees.

1. This story is about birds that lose their feathers, or_____ .

2. When does molting usually happen? _____

    _____

3. Write the sentence in paragraph four that tells what a mother eagle does.

    _____

    _____

4. Why do you think fall is a good time to grow new feathers?

    _____

    _____

5. What is a word in paragraph three that means "to take the place of the old"?

    _____

6. Write the contractions found in paragraph three. _____

Name _____

Where do insects go in winter?

     At a summer picnic, flies and ants will bother you. In the winter, they are hard to find. Where do insects go when cold weather comes?

     Most of them die as the weather gets colder. But they leave their eggs behind. The eggs are hidden in plants or underground. They do not hatch until they sense the signs of spring.

     For example, almost all flies die in the fall. They lay their eggs near trash cans. A female fly will lay 150 eggs at once. When they hatch in the spring, the new flies eat the garbage. Flies grow up in just a few weeks.

     Some insects hide during the winter. You might find ants and crickets under some tree bark. When the sun shines on a warm winter day, they step out.

     Bees live in their hives. They eat the honey they gathered all summer long. Moths may live in their cocoons, which protect them.

     Some insects travel south, just like birds. Monarch butterflies will travel 1,500 miles for warmth. Ladybugs also head south. They know exactly when to turn around and head north again!

1. This story is about where insects go in _____ weather.

2. What happens to flies in the winter?

    _____

3. Write the sentence in paragraph four that tells about ants in winter.

    _____

    _____

4. What "signs of spring" would tell insects to come out of hiding or to hatch?

    _____

5. What is a word in paragraph five that means "a silky covering for moths"?

    _____

6. Write the plural of these words:

    fly: _____   butterfly:_____

    moth: _____   hive:_____

Name _____

Do fish sleep?

Fish sleep with their eyes open. Maybe you've noticed that they don't blink. They cannot close their eyes. Fish have no eyelids.

If a fish is very still, it is most likely sleeping. At times, fish will rest their bodies on the bottom of their fish tank. In the ocean, they may lean against a rock. Or they may lie in the sand at the bottom of the water. Fish rest their bodies, just as people do.

Fish tend to be light sleepers. The least noise or movement will wake them. Fish do have ears. They are hidden inside their heads. They also have tiny feelers that pick up movement. They can even sense footsteps on land.

Dolphins seem to sleep with one eye open. They sleep on just one side of their bodies at a time. They need to breathe air. So they must sleep near the surface of the water.

Dolphins sleep two to three hours a day. They rest in groups. A lookout dolphin watches for danger.

1. This story is about how fish_____ .

2. What are some ways you can tell if a fish is sleeping?

   _____

   _____

3. Which paragraph tells about the eyes of a fish?

   _____

4. Why do you think dolphins are light sleepers?

   _____

   _____

5. What is a word in paragraph one that means "took note of" or "was aware of"?

   _____

6. What is the plural of fish? _____

Name _____

Why do dogs wag their tails?

    Dogs can't talk with words. But they let you know how they feel with their bodies. When a dog wags its tail, it feels good. It is telling you it likes you and wants your attention.

    Dogs use their tails to send messages. A big dog might come near a smaller one's bone. The little dog will raise its tail in the air. It's like saying, "This is my space. Don't come any closer."

    If you scold your dog, its tail might drop and curl between its legs. This means, "Please don't yell at me. I'm sorry."

    Dogs use other parts of their bodies to show their feelings. A dog might jump on you with its tail wagging. It would be saying, "Let's play."

    But if a dog growls in its throat, it is saying, "Stand back. I'm in a bad mood." Stay away or you may be bitten!

    Some dogs don't want you to look them straight in the eyes. They think you are asking for trouble.

1. This story is about why dogs_____ .

2. What do dogs send with their tails?

   _____

   _____

3. Which paragraph tells you what a dog is saying when it growls?

   _____

4. What do you think a dog's ears do when it is happy?

   _____

5. If a dog wants to be noticed, he wants your _____ .

6. What are the contractions in paragraph two?

   _____

Name _____

Why do mosquitoes bite?

The mosquito is a real pest. It may hum in your ear when you sleep. It may bite you. Then you get those red sores that itch.

Only female mosquitoes bite. They do this on purpose. They want your blood. They suck out small amounts of blood. Then they feed their eggs with it.

Mosquitoes bite with a set of sharp needles. These needles are part of their mouths. In all, there are six of these sharp parts in a mosquito. No wonder a bite hurts!

At the time of the bite, the mosquito spits juices. These juices flow into your wound. They are called saliva. The saliva mixes with your blood and thins it. If the blood were thick, it would be too hard for the mosquito to drink.

The saliva is what makes a bite swell and itch. Most people are allergic to it. Saliva is like poison. Your body sends cells to fight this enemy. Think of it as a war going on under your skin. That's why your skin turns red.

Mosquitoes carry germs. They have been known to carry certain diseases. Some towns spray their neighborhoods at night to kill these pests and prevent disease.

1. This story is about the pest known as the _____ .

2. What kind of mosquitoes bite? _____

3. Which paragraph tells about the juices a mosquito spits? _____

4. What does a mosquito use to get blood from your body?

_____

5. What is a word in paragraph four that means "the juices a mosquito spits"?

_____

6. Write the plural for each of these words:

   mosquito:_____   needle:_____

   mix: _____   disease: _____

Name _____

Why do dogs bury bones?

At one time, dogs were not pets. They were wild and lived outdoors. Food was hard to find. When they found a weak animal, they killed it. But they couldn't eat the animal all at once. So they saved some of it for the next meal.

Other dogs wanted the food. To avoid a fight, dogs would bury what they could not eat. The bones were buried, too. In this way, all traces of the animal were hidden.

Of course, today, most dogs are fed by their owners. They don't have to hunt. But they still have the urge to bury bones and dig holes. They are born with this desire. It is called "instinct."

Instinct is strong in animals. It tells them what to do. Children can talk to their parents and learn what to do. But most animals grow up faster. They need a set of inner thoughts. These thoughts tell them things they need to know.

Dogs will turn in circles before they lie down. This is also an instinct. They think they are smoothing a pile of leaves for their bed.

1. This story is about strange things dogs do by _____ .

2. What is instinct? _____

    _____

3. Which paragraph tells how dogs of long ago got their food? _____

4. If a pet dog was lost in a forest for ten days, how do you think it would get its food?

    _____

    _____

5. What is a word in paragraph four that means "within yourself"?

    _____

6. Write the past tense of these verbs:

    bury: _____   find: _____

    feed: _____   save: _____

Should a dog's nose be wet?

Most of the time, it is normal for a dog to have a wet nose. The nose is one of the few places where a dog sweats.

People have small pores in their skin. When you are hot, you sweat through these openings. A dog gets warm, too. But it cannot sweat like you do. A dog has to cool down through its nose and mouth.

As sweat leaves the dog's nose, it forms tiny drops. This moisture is what makes the nose wet. It keeps the dog cool.

Dogs also lose heat through their mouths. They do this by panting. This cools the dog down. A dog can pant for a long time. It doesn't have to be old or out of shape to pant.

A dog's wet nose also helps it to smell. The wetness seems to trap odors. That is why dogs have such a keen sense of smell.

Finally, dogs lick their noses and make them wet. This is just like a child who licks his lips because they feel dry.

So it is O.K. for your dog to have a wet nose.

1. This story is about. _____

_____

2. What are two ways a dog gets rid of heat? _____

_____

3. Which paragraph talks about a dog's sense of smell?

_____

4. How can you help your pet dog to stay cool?

_____

_____

5. What is a word in paragraph six that means "last of all"?

_____

6. Write the homonyms for these words:

pours: _____   cents:_____

knows:_____   dew:_____

What is an echo?

Stand in an empty room that has no furniture. Say a short phrase. You will hear the sound of your own voice after you stop talking. That sound is an echo.

This will also happen if you are in the mountains. Call out "hello." You will hear the sound return.

Each time you speak, your words are carried across sound waves. These waves bring your words to your friends. They move just like waves in an ocean.

When sound waves hit a large object, they may bounce back to you. That is the echo you hear. It is like throwing a ball at a wall and catching it when it bounces back.

The echo can be heard in an empty room because there are no other objects to absorb the sound. If the room has chairs, beds, and tables, they disturb the echo. It can't be heard as well.

If you speak softly, the echo won't be heard. The sound waves are too weak. If you talk facing a door, there won't be an echo. The door is too small to bounce the waves back to you.

1. This story is about hearing your voice come back as an _____ .

2. How do the words you speak reach your friends? _____

   _____

3. Write the sentence in paragraph four that compares an echo to a ball.

   _____

   _____

4. What other kinds of sounds do you think would make an echo?

   _____

5. What is a word in paragraph five that means "to soak up"?

   _____

6. Write two words in paragraph four that rhyme.

   _____

Name _____

What is a sonic boom?

Sometimes an airplane goes so fast it makes a sound like thunder. Boom! This noise is a sonic boom. Sonic means "sound."

You know that water moves in waves. Air also moves in waves. Of course, we can't see these air waves but they are there.

When a plane travels fast, it disturbs these waves of air. They get pushed away from the plane. If a plane goes faster than the speed of sound, the waves pile up behind the plane. They tumble into each other. Then they send out a giant shock wave.

On the ground, we can hear this shock wave as a boom. The noise might be so loud that windows could break. Your house might even shake. But the waves won't hurt you.

Planes no longer fly faster than sound when they are near cities. They don't want to damage homes.

1. This story is about a kind of noise called a _____ .

2. What four kinds of waves are talked about in the story?

   _____

   _____

3. Write the sentence in paragraph three that tells what happens when a plane goes faster than sound.

   _____

   _____

4. How many sonic booms do you think a plane makes while it flies faster than sound?

   _____

5. What is a word in paragraph three that means "to upset"?

   _____

6. What are two compound words in paragraph one?

   _____

Why do stars twinkle?

On a clear night, the stars seem to twinkle. It looks like their lights turn on and off or get brighter. Stars do not really twinkle. The air above our Earth causes this. You see, the air's movement bends the light from the stars. When the light reaches us, we see it bend. That is what we call a twinkle.

If you could see the stars from outer space, their lights would never fade. You would also see that stars don't have points. Stars are round balls of light, like our sun. They always shine with a steady light.

The stars shine day and night. But our sun, which is a star, blocks this light. In the day, the sun's light is so bright that it keeps you from seeing the stars. But there are stars above you at all times.

Some stars are brighter than others. Perhaps they are closer to Earth. Or their extreme heat makes them glow more brightly.

1. This story is about how the stars seem to _____ .

2. What causes stars to appear to twinkle? _____

    _____

3. Write the sentence in paragraph two that tells what shape stars are.

    _____

    _____

4. Why do you think we can see the sun during the day?

    _____

    _____

5. What is a word in paragraph four that means "very great"?

    _____

6. What is a homonym for the word "their"?

    _____

How are clouds formed?

Clouds in the sky look white or grey. They have a shape and can be seen. Yet you could put your hand right through them. Clouds cannot be felt.

Clouds are formed from tiny water drops that float in the air. The water was once on the earth. It was in lakes, ponds, and pools. But warm breezes blew over the water. They picked up some of the water and carried it high in the air. Warm air always rises.

As the air rises, it cools down. Then it releases the water drops. They stick together and form clouds. These clouds move with the wind. Sometimes they will hit a pocket of warm air. Then the water drops split apart. This makes the cloud change shape. The drops might form a whole new cloud. Or they might move to a different part of the same cloud. Some of them may disappear.

The wind can also break the cloud apart with its force. That is why clouds are always changing the way they look. When a cloud has too many water drops to hold, it will release them. This is rain.

1. This story is about clouds that form from _____ .

2. What kind of air lifts the water from the earth?

    _____

    _____

3. Which paragraph tells where the water drops once were? _____

4. Why do you think that on some days there are no clouds.

    _____

    _____

5. What is a word in paragraph four that means "let go of"?

    _____

6. Write the past tense of these words:

    blow: _____   feel: _____

    pick: _____   carry: _____

Name _____

What is an earthquake?

During an earthquake, the ground shakes. Houses wobble back and forth. Cans fall off the shelves in stores. This movement lasts only a few seconds. But it can do a lot of damage.

Earthquakes happen underground. The Earth has a crust, just like a pie does. The crust is made from huge sheets of rock. The crust floats on top of very hot liquids and more rocks. These liquids are always moving. They cause pressure to build.

The sheets of rock feel this pressure. It makes them push against each other. This goes on for some time. The place where two large sheets of rock push against each other is a fault. Often it can be seen as a crack in the Earth's surface.

Finally the pressure is too much. All the rocks in that area shift at once. We feel this swaying for miles. This is an earthquake. After it happens, the rocks should be all right for awhile. Then the pressure will build again.

The most famous earthquake took place in San Francisco in 1906. It destroyed most of that city.

1. This story is about a strong shaking called an _____ .

2. What pushes against each other?

   _____

3. Write the sentence in paragraph two that tells what the Earth's crust is like.

   _____

   _____

4. What do you think an earthquake would sound like?

   _____

   _____

5. What is a word in paragraph one that means "to teeter back and forth"?

   _____

6. Write two compound words from paragraph two.

   _____

Name _____

What are comets?

Comets are made up of water, dust, and gases. They float through space. Chunks of ice form at the comet's core. This core is quite large. As the comet moves, it attracts rocks and dust. These loose objects follow behind the comet. They form the tail.

Comets travel through space in a fixed path. The path is called an orbit. A comet's orbit often leads to the sun. Sooner or later the comet circles the sun. Then it moves away. After many years, it turns around and heads back for the sun. This may happen once every 75, 200, or 500 years.

When the comet is near the sun, some of its ice melts. This makes a kind of glow. It is this glow that can be seen. It might look like a bright star.

Comets move at speeds of thousands of miles per hour. Yet, to the eye, they seem to stand still. Each time a comet circles the sun, it loses some of its ice. Someday it will melt and disappear.

1. This story is about space bodies called_____ .

2. What are the two parts of a comet? _____

   _____

3. Which paragraph tells about the comet's path? _____

4. What do you think the space temperature must be like to hold the comet together?

   _____

   _____

5. What is a word in paragraph one that means "the center part"?

   _____

6. Write a compound word in paragraph four.

   _____

Name _____

How long have we used bikes?

The first bikes were built almost 200 years ago. They had two wheels. They were held together by a curved bar.

These bikes had no pedals. To ride one, you had to push it along the ground with your feet. These bikes were like scooters. They were called hobby horses.

Pedals came about 50 years later. But the bikes had a big problem. The wheels were made from wood. Think how bumpy the ride must have been. In fact, they were called "boneshakers."

By the 1860's, rubber wheels were used. But these bikes still looked strange. The front wheel was huge. The two rear wheels were tiny. The seat was high in the air. You needed a ladder to reach it. If you fell, it was a long way to the ground.

The bike of today was first built about 100 years ago. Each year, more bikes are built than cars.

1. This story is about _____ .

2. What were two names for early bikes?

   _____

3. Which paragraph tells about a big improvement in the wheels?

   _____

4. What are some ways in which bikes could be better than cars?

   _____

   _____

5. What is a word in paragraph four that means "in the back; behind"?

   _____

6. Write the past tense of these verbs.

   build: _____   have: _____

   hold: _____   make: _____

Name _____

Why do people like diamonds?

Diamonds are very costly. There are stones that are more rare. But there are no stones harder than diamonds.

A diamond is part of certain rocks that are found deep in the earth. Most of them come from South Africa. They are made from carbon. When the carbon is found, it does not sparkle. It looks like a piece of glass. The rock must be carefully cut and polished. Special tools are needed to do this. After much polishing, the diamond takes shape.

This stone is cut so it has many sides. The sides are called facets. These facets are what make a diamond shine. They reflect light and break it into many colors. That is why a diamond looks like it contains a rainbow.

The first diamond engagement ring was given in the 1400's. A duke gave one to his love. Since then, a diamond ring has come to mean a promise to marry someone.

1. This story is about the _____ stone, the diamond.

2. What does a diamond look like in the ground?

   _____

   _____

3. Which paragraph tells about diamond rings?

   _____

4. What other stones do you think are costly?

   _____

5. What is a word in paragraph four that means "a promise to marry"?

   _____

6. Write the plurals of these words:

   stone: _____   facet: _____

   diamond: _____   side: _____

Name _____

How can people travel underground?

People drive cars on the ground and fly planes in the sky. But some people travel underground. They use subways.

Subways are long tunnels under the earth. Electric trains move through them. To board these trains, you first find a subway station. Then you walk down some steps to get to the tracks. When the train pulls up, you must move fast. The doors open and close very quickly.

You can use the subway the same way you use a car or bus. Subways will take you to work, to stores, and to see friends. But you must know when to exit.

The first subway was built in London in 1863. The trains burned coal for fuel. This made them quite dirty. The first subway in the United States was built in Boston in 1897. But New York has the most complete subway system.

At least 65 cities in the world now use subways. None of them use coal any longer. They are all electric.

1. This story is about traveling underground on _____ .

2. What are subways? _____

    _____

3. Which paragraph tells how to board a subway train? _____

4. Why do you think subways would be good for a city?

    _____

    _____

5. What is a word in paragraph two that means "a covered passageway"?

    _____

6. Write an antonym from the story for each of these words:

    clean: _____   close: _____

Name _____

What sport is played all over the world?

In the United States, we like to play baseball and football. But the best-loved sport in the world is soccer. Soccer is played in 140 countries.

People like to watch soccer games. One soccer match had a crowd of 200,000 people. That's as many people as live in a medium-sized city.

Soccer rules are simple. Even small children can play. It is much safer than football. All you need is the right kind of ball. Almost any playing field will do. Players try to score goals by kicking the ball across the field. They also bounce the ball off parts of their bodies. Two teams play against each other.

Brazil has some of the best soccer teams. They have been world champions three times. The trophy they receive for being the best is called the World Cup.

Fans often like to run onto the soccer field after a game. To keep them away, one field has water between the players and the fans. If they want to reach the players, the fans must swim across seven feet of water.

1. This story is about a sport called _____ .

2. How many countries play soccer?

   _____

3. Which paragraph tells the rules of soccer? _____

4. How do you know that soccer is popular?

   _____

   _____

5. What is a word in paragraph three that means "points that are scored"?

   _____

6. Write two other forms of the word "play" from paragraph three

   _____

Name _____

Who first made ice cream?

The first ice cream was the dessert of kings. It was made from snow. Slaves would run to the mountains and gather snow. Back in the palace, they would add fruit or honey. Roman kings liked ice cream.

The Chinese made ice cream, too. Theirs contained milk. Years later, in Italy, ice cream was first made with cream. It was called the "flower of milk." The chefs would not tell anyone how they made this treat.

A man named Mr. Green made the first ice cream soda. It was an accident. He had a booth at a fair. He sold drinks. One day he ran out of cream. So he added ice cream to water and syrup. The soda was a big hit.

At another fair, two men were talking. One sold ice cream. The other sold waffles. They decided to combine their booths. The ice cream was poured into the waffles. That was the first ice cream cone.

1. This story is about where _____ was first eaten.

2. From what was the first ice cream made?_____

   _____

3. Which paragraph tells about how the soda got started? _____

4. How is today's ice cream different from what the Romans ate?

   _____

   _____

5. What is a word in paragraph one that means "a treat after a meal"?

   _____

6. Write words from paragraph two that rhyme with these words:

   dream: _____   nice: _____

   silk: _____   power: _____

Who wrote the first books?

Books as we know them have existed for about 500 years. But ancient people also wrote down their thoughts. Writings that are 4,000 years old have been found.

These writings were carved on pieces of clay. The pieces were called tablets. A piece of iron, called a chisel, was the pen.

In Egypt they learned how to use plants for paper. The plants were tall reeds. They were called papyrus. The reeds were cut and pressed into thin sheets. To store them, the sheets were rolled on sticks. These rolled sheets were called scrolls. Scrolls that are 24 feet long and 10 inches wide have been found.

Books with parchment paper came about 300 A.D. Parchment was made from animal skins. The skins were sewn together. The writers used pens called quills.

All books were written by hand until the mid-1400's. At that time, the first printing press was made. At last, more than one copy of a book could be printed at the same time.

1. This story is about how long _____ have existed.

2. What did people in Egypt use for paper? _____

   _____

3. Write the sentence in paragraph four that tells from what parchment was made.

   _____

   _____

4. What do you think school was like in the year 1,000 B.C.?

   _____

   _____

5. What is a word in paragraph one that means "very old"?

   _____

6. Write the plural for these words:

   thought: _____   piece: _____

28

PAGE 1: 1) colds 2) sore throat, sneezing, coughing, being tired, watery eyes 3) The germ is a virus. 4) doctor 5) protected 6) nose, sore, air

PAGE 2: 1) rest or sleep 2) they get stronger 3) four 4) You would probably miss the ball more often: you wouldn't have much concentration; you might even collapse 5) grouchy 6) energy, remember

PAGE 3: 1) bones 2) old age 3) You are born with 270 bones. 4) Bones must grow so we can become taller and bigger; otherwise, we would stay the same size as at birth. 5) twigs 6) bones, bony

PAGE 4: 1) strong/hard, healthy 2) enamel is good; plaque is bad 3) Yet your teeth are harder than your bones! 4) dentist drills, then fills them with strong material 5) pressure 6) peanut, maybe

PAGE 5: 1) heart 2) It must send blood to each part of your body. 3) five 4) keeps you alive by pumping blood 5) exercise 6) faster, slower

PAGE 6: 1) sneeze 2) The nose catches all the unwanted particles. 3) dust and dirt float through the air 4) stay away from whatever causes the problem 5) clog 6) sometimes

PAGE 7: 1) heals 2) cells 3) three 4) The limb might be crooked. It might be difficult to move the limb even though it was healed. 5) connect 6) doctors, casts, arms, legs

PAGE 8: 1) protect 2) keep sweat out of eyes 3) Most of your body heat is lost through your head in the winter. 4) wear a covering on your head (hat, scarf, etc.) 5) pressure 6) hair

PAGE 9: 1) owls, bats 2) Owls eat mice and other small critters. 3) four 4) they can run fast, can get into holes, can hide in corners and tight places 5) handy 6) eyesight, footsteps

PAGE 10: 1) molting 2) at the end of summer 3) A mother eagle will pull out her own feathers to line her nest. 4) With winter coming, birds need the best set of feathers possible. 5) replace 6) couldn't, doesn't

PAGE 11: 1) cold 2) they die but leave behind eggs 3) You might find ants and crickets under some tree bark. 4) warmer weather, more sunshine, smells in the air, longer evenings 5) cocoons 6) flies, moths, butterflies, hives

PAGE 12: 1) sleep 2) not moving; resting at bottom of tank; leans against a rock 3) one 4) They have to be alert for enemies, wake up often and get air. 5) noticed 6) fish or fishes

PAGE 13: 1) wag their tails 2) messages 3) five 4) perk up or stand up 5) attention 6) It's, Don't

PAGE 14: 1) mosquito 2) female 3) four 4) needles in its mouth 5) saliva 6) mosquitoes, needles, mixes, diseases

PAGE 15: 1) instinct 2) Instinct is a set of inner thoughts that tell animals how to do something without them learning it. 3) one 4) It would probably use its hunting instinct and kill a smaller animal for food. 5) inner 6) buried, fed, found, saved

PAGE 16: 1) Why a dog's nose is wet 2) through its nose and mouth 3) five 4) keep it inside or make sure it has shade: give it plenty of water 5) finally 6) pores, nose, sense, do

PAGE 17: 1) echo 2) They travel by sound waves. 3) It is like throwing a ball at a wall and catching it when it bounces back. 4) airplane noise, barking dogs, a gun, etc. 5) absorb 6) ball, wall

PAGE 18: 1) sonic boom 2) sound waves, water waves, air waves, shock waves 3) If a plane goes faster than the speed of sound, the waves pile up behind the plane. 4) It would keep making a series of booms until it slowed down. You would probably hear only the one above you. 5) disturbs 6) sometimes, airplane

PAGE 19: 1) twinkle 2) the air above the earth 3) Stars are round balls of light, like our sun. 4) it is close to Earth and is very bright 5) extreme 6) there

PAGE 20: 1) tiny water drops in the air 2) warm air 3) two 4) no warm breezes come by to pick up water: water drops may be so few and small that there aren't enough to stick together and form a cloud 5) release 6) blew, picked, felt, carried

PAGE 21: 1) earthquake 2) huge sheets of rock in the earth's crust 3) The earth has a crust, just like a pie does. 4) You probably wouldn't hear actual sounds in the ground. You would hear buildings and loose objects shake. 5) wobble 6) Earthquakes, underground

PAGE 22: 1) comets 2) core and tail 3) two 4) very cold 5) core 6) someday

PAGE 23: 1) the first bikes 2) hobby horse, boneshakers 3) four 4) you can squeeze into tight places in traffic; parking a bike takes less space: don't have to spend money on gas: doesn't cause pollution 5) rear 6) built, held, had, made

PAGE 24: 1) hardest 2) It looks like a piece of glass. 3) four 4) rubies, emeralds, pearls, sapphires 5) engagement 6) stones, diamonds, facets, sides

PAGE 25: 1) subways 2) long tunnels under the earth with trains moving through them 3) two 4) cities are crowded with buildings so putting the trains underground saves space; they are clean, they don't burn gas 5) tunnels 6) dirty, open

PAGE 26: 1) soccer 2) 140 3) three 4) by all the countries that play soccer; by the size of the crowds 5) goals 6) playing, players

PAGE 27: 1) ice cream 2) snow and fruit or honey 3) three 4) ours uses cream or milk and comes in lots of flavors 5) dessert 6) cream, milk, ice, flower

PAGE 28: 1) books 2) They used plants that were tall reeds called papyrus. 3) Parchment was made from animal skins. 4) School was probably a single room. Students would gather scrolls: teacher would unroll scrolls and teach them to read. 5) ancient 6) thoughts, pieces